WORDS OF INSPIRATION

From the Power of my Pen

WORDS OF INSPIRATION

From the Power of my Pen

WRITTEN BY

EARNESTINE SMART

DESIGN BY

MARY KAY SANTO

To order additional copies of this book, contact:
Xlibris Corporation
1-888-795-4274
www.Xlibris.com
Orders@Xlibris.com
34192

Contents

With love, I dedicate this book to my family and friends.
To those who have inspired my words
and supported my efforts,
I thank you.

Through Inspiration My Heart Sings

As I sit here in the calmness
I'm captured by the inspiration
That flows through gently to my mind
Such words of wisdom and understanding appear
Unto me to be soaked up in the thirst
Of hunger that I so graciously taste
To be able to digest the very substance
As I look around after being sedated
In the knowing of the Spirit of truth
As I write somewhere in the subject that
One will be captured by the words of wisdom
That has been written and the self-healing
Be passed to the Inner feeling
To make the heart happy
And be able to see and feel the joy
As the encouraging words
Send a message of consolation
Of one trial to set the mind and soul free
As the cycles of life's journey continues
To unfold the many secrets of self
To discover much of the mind's mystery
And sense such beauty
That's imbedded in one's being—self
Like the lily that floats on its pad
Surrounded by the mirror of water that reflects its depth
So goes life in all its channels
How gracious and loving are all these
Unseen circumstances
As its surprises of bubbles begin to surface
And burst exploring in particles
Of translucent colors of the spectrum
That ascends into the horizon in question
Of how well do I know me?

Acknowledgment

It is with great appreciation that I wish to thank Mary Kay Santo, Linda and Phil Hutton, and Jo Dee and Moise Devillier for their help and support in the production of this publication. They have allowed my dream to take flight and become a reality. Without their efforts, this would not have been possible. For this I am so grateful. Thank you.

Introduction

As a writer of my inner feelings, an emotional being has brought me to a point that I can look back over my life and see how the Lord has blessed me with much abundance. He inscribes upon my heart the wisdom that I am greatly gifted with to be able to write poetry. I just let my mind be guided and witness by the power of my pen, the words that are bestowed upon me. The taste of poetry begins to flow. There is so much joy to be captured by the mind and heart of each reader. It's an interpretation of true feelings, different events, and soul-searching in faith. I hope it can be of great consolation to many readers, family, and friends brought together with love and understanding.

My Flower Garden

As I walk through my garden
My flowers seem to know
How much I really love them
And watch them as they grow.

I water them with love
And feed them with care.
And when the harvest comes
They blossom everywhere.

I have three stags
Hung on three trees
Their antlers seem
To reach out to me

As I walk among the trees
And enjoy the gentleness of the breeze
That whispers softly through the leaves.

The ground cover it seems to know
The trail that it shows grow.
This garden is a special place
Where I can walk or kneel and pray.

I can spend five minutes or an hour
And to know He's with me
I feel His presence by the visitation of His holy power.

This is the Joy my garden unfolds
As I take my garden stroll.

Memories of You

Looking at your picture
Reminds me of you-
The places we went
And the things we used to do.

The days we spent together
Was happy as could be
Now I'm all alone,
With just your memory

A picture to remind me
Of what we once had.
Now I think of you
And my heart feels sad.

We used to laugh and dance
And hold each other tight
We even strolled along the seashore
Beneath the bright moonlight.

Now I'm left with your memories
And so many lonely nights
And with the thoughts of losing you
I lay there and cry.

I'll keep on living
With all these lonely tears
And in my heart
I'll always cherish the happiness
We shared through all the years.

Words Spoken from the Heart

In loving memory of
Evelyn Sullivan

I'd seen you many times
And finally we met.
Now you're in my heart,
Never to forget

It was very nice to meet you
And now that you were known,
Your precious memories
Will live on and on

As your golden days come to end
Of a new horizon,

Sleep in heavenly peace.

Always Remembered

The way you brighten my day,
You are my sunshine.
When raindrops fall,
Whenever I need you,
You hear my call.
I am so happy that I know you;
You change my world from misty to blue.

Time will bring about a change,
But my love will remain.
With you I see sunshine again.
I'm happy that we're friends.
With you sunshine has no end.

It's okay when skies are blue
For my sunshine, you are my love.

Ghetto Woman

Ghetto woman, I've told you once
I'm am telling you twice,
Get out of here, take my advice.
The road may be long, rocky, and hard,
Reach for the impossible and trust in God.
Find yourself in the city of lights
You will become a star shinning bright.
Mixing among the kings and queens
Being recognized on every scene.
Never forgetting where you have been
Making a difference to women and men
Ghetto woman, you are my friend.

From the Work I've Done

Nothing seems to matter
When nighttime comes around
Just a place to lay my head
So I can settle down

The evenings comes so fast
And days really go
Before I realize
The night creeps in before I know

When morning rolls around
As the peak of dawn appears
The best of my life to you
Is sincere

From the yesterdays I had
I know how sincere life can be
When you know
You really care

America the Beautiful Sweet Liberty

I sense her cry as she calls for me
As I hear her softly in the wind
I'll answer her, I'm her true friend
I'm a soldier going to war.

I have my armor on
The battlefield is waiting
The fighting has long begun
I have no fear of tomorrow
Because inside of me
I'm my own hero.
To my country 'tis of thee
To which it stands
When the war is over
I know I'll be free.

I can say to Sweet Liberty
And to the flag that stands
As she waves her banner proud,
America is beautiful to me.

America, you are beautiful
I'll say to her again
I know she stands for me
The soldier that I am.

I'm a soldier going to war.

I

I have my armor on
The battlefield is waiting
The fighting has long begun
I have no fear of tomorrow
Because inside of me
I'm my own hero.
To my country 'tis of thee
To which it stands
When the war is over
I know I'll be free.

I can say to sweet liberty
And to the flag that stands
As she waves her banner proud
America is beautiful to me.

America, you are beautiful
I'll say to her again
I know she stands for me
The soldier that I am

I Owe You

To you my love I owe
So much to give and more
For understanding and peace of mind
For me it was hard to find, until I met you.

Laughter begins to be my friend
Joy and sunshine fill right in
It was you, my love
That brought me happiness
Through it all, our love was blessed.

Let My Love Heal

Let me learn to love again
And my tears be washed away
Let me not feel the hurt
That was only yesterday

I must consider this heart of mine
For my love is very deep
Like the bud of a rose
For you my love I'll keep

Let my love light shine for you
Like the best of gold you will find
Purer than the silver
Then you can see
My love light shining bright

Brighten Up Your World

Live like the world is yours
A place you can call your own
Live like tomorrow is here
And the sky is yours alone

Live like you've danced the night away
And the sky was clear of its stars
And the sun took the sight of the moon

Live this way and you'll smile
Showing nothing else but love
Your troubled mind will vanish
And brighten up your world.

A Wonderful Sister

I'm glad that you're my sister
Because you're one of a special kind
A jewel among a field of flowers
That's rare and hard to find.

I think of you all the time
And wish that you could be
Not so far across the miles
Just a little closer here to me.

I think of you so very much
More often than you know
How glad I am that you're my sister
And I love you so.

I'm in Love with You!

I'll wipe away your every tear,
After all the Hurt I've put you through.
There's no need to worry no more
'Cause I'll take good care of you.

I love you, baby, I'll keep a smile on your face,
I'll work seven days if that's what it takes
To keep you happy and be your loving man.

I love you, honey, and I want the whole world to know.
I'll give you flowers and a ring to show,
My love for you will always be strong.
There's nothing that can make me do wrong.

Take my love, honey; I'll give it all to you.
You're a dream I've searched for my whole life through.
Say you will marry me, darling, and accept this ring,
I'll give you good loving and the best of everything.

I'll reach out for the moon, way up in the sky,
Stand beneath the starlight, and dry the
Teardrops from your eyes

And before the sun rises at the break of each day,
I'll get down on my knees and pray
That our love will last always.

A Lifetime of Dreams

When I go walking through my mind
I see those old familiar faces
And places I used to know,
Places I don't go anymore

How happy were those days
In so many ways
No comparison can be
Of the days that I see
When I go walking through my mind

A Sentimental journey
Is what I am looking for
A stroll on the beach
Beneath the moon and stars

I don't need a fancy car to drive,
Just a hand to hold
This means more to me
Than silver and gold
When I go walking through my mind
Just the two of us make such lovely pair.

A Difference in My Day

Today as I awake
At the dawn of the morning
Being clothed in a right frame of mind,
And inward thoughts to be
Thankful for life alone,
To be able to take in a breath of air
Lord, I thank thee.

To look around the great outside
And focus on the sky alone
And know the earth beneath my feet,
So great was His plan.

Today is a different day.
One I've never seen
And to the best in life I can
Because it's not a dream.

I'm thankful because
I know I'm not alone
With so much love
He's given me
I feel deep inside.

I can tell the world
He's real and He's alive.
Almighty God,
He is Jesus Christ, my Lord.

Your Day Will Come

So blinded by your love that I could not see
You took my love and you shattered my dreams.
How could you treat me this way?
How could you be so mean?

I was so blindly in love with you
You had me sitting home all alone,
Wishing you'd call me on the telephone.

My love for you was so sincere
With you by my side, I had no fear.

The only motion running through my head
Was wrapped up in your loving arms instead.

I never thought that you would cheat on me
A love like yours seemed meant to be.

Your kisses were sweeter than wine
Like the sweetest of grapes from the vine.

Loving you was all I wanted,
Oh, how I was disappointed.

A notion that I made my own
The night I said you could take me home.

Whom Do You Blame?

Who do you see?
When you're looking at me
Don't be judgmental
Just let me be.

Don't worry about the color of my skin,
Feel my pulse, my heart beats within!

Who do you see?
When you look into my eyes
Can you see the tears I have shed?
Don't you know I have cried?

Who do you see?
When you are looking at me
Don't take away my pride
Let me be free
I'm just a human and I want to be free.

Can you see it in my eyes?
When you're looking at me?

Who Am I?

Today, I'm who I am.
Tomorrow is not a promise
Of what I will be.

But while I am in the present
I'll be the best
Of all I can be!

If I make it through today
And awake to the morning dawn,
Yesterday became the past of what I learned.

The presence still remains
And the past has come and gone.

Then who I thought I wanted to be
Was already inside of me.
Who I am!

When We Sail Away

Someday
When my ship sets sail
Out there on the sea
I'll sail away

Across the big blue sea
Miles on miles will I be
Away from dry land
Out there in the blue
Just me and you

The seas will roar a song
That only it can hum
And to listen to the waves
Is all we will hear

Just to have you close to me
There's no place I'd rather be
Sailing away with you is okay

Just another day
Out there on the bay
Is where I'd like to stay
Just being here with you
Makes my days
And my dreams come true

A Closer Look at the Peacock Through Stained Glass

As I look through the window
At the peacock as he struts
He must be awful proud of himself
Very much

To walk along the riverside
Where the sun creates a gleam
Upon the river
Water of the fallen rain
A rainbow can be seen
The little sailboat afar,

He rests there content
While the trees along the bank
Bow with branches bent
As the vines entangles
With the grass that grows

As he steps so proudly in the grass
He spreads his fan to show
The beauty of its colors
As if he really knows
It's undeniably beautiful
As he's on the go

When the Day Is Done

Searching through the night
To find a place to rest
Toiling from the day
That I've done my best
Nothing seems to matter
But my life must go on
And I too must be at ease
When the day is done

I'll rise to the light of the breaking dawn
To find a peace in mind when the day is done
Strengthened by my will from my soul within

What a difference to compare
To the night then day
When the day is done, I can go my way.

When I'm with You

When I'm with you, my love
My world is brighter in so many ways.
Bring me the joy and sunshine
On my gloomiest day.

In your voice there's music to my ears
Soothing sweet melodies I love to hear.
Rhythms that last me hours long!
Turning the tune it's a love song.
This is how you make me feel
And to me, my love, I know your love is real.

And I'm in love with you.
When my world is in a mush
You changed my life.

Just one kiss brings out the best in me
When I'm with you, my love.

What Your Love Means to Me

With you in my life there is so much love to give.
I'll cherish your love for as long as I live.
For better or worse, in everything
Oh, how wonderful what true love can bring.

The happiness I've found since you've been around.
My love for you is chained and bound.

To cherish your love you so gently give.
It flourishes in my heart with such a thrill.
Since the day I met you,
You've been one of a kind.
Your loving ways just blow my mind.
As long as the stars and moon shine above,
Together we'll share each other's love.
With me loving you and you loving me.
It's the way true love is supposed to be.

Here's to you, darling.
May we never forget
Our love was abound the first time we met.
Feel my love, know my heart.
We will never be apart.

What Love Will Do

He who created the universe
And placed the moon, sun, and the stars
In all the wonders of the world
He made us who we are.

Look into a garden of flowers of different colors.
How great His plan with all the beauty
They portrayed was passed on to man.

It was love from the very beginning
A love that knows no ending
A love so very meek and mild
A love that was born a child
A love that walked and lived among men
A love who taught them of their sin
When all seems well, maybe it's really not,
There just may be something we forgot.

How my Savior went away
Out on a hillside to pray
He did not need a house or home
He was God Almighty on the throne.

But so much love He had for me
That He gave His life upon the cross.

So that my soul would not be lost
Look at each other today and say,
This I know is true indeed, He has risen

No grave could hold his body down
He lives in me and you
He died for us all.

What a Beautiful Mind

For an imaginary thought
Of someone like you
For me to visualize
Before my very eyes
Can be so real and not be true

My eyes had seen
That look upon your face
My heart knew what you were.
What awesome trace
What an image to be seen
Of all the people in the world

You appeared in the scene
You came along and echoed sweet sounds
That could be heard all around
A touch as gentle as the morning breeze

A look I shall never forget
Then you vanished like a shadow
Just as you came you went
Only to be captured by a beautiful mind

America, I Love You

No other land I'd rather be
That's grand as ours alone
Whose song we sing of liberty
As sweet as our own

With stars and stripes flowing
Endlessly of red, white, and blue
This is America that says, I Love You

America you're beautiful,
My song will always be
Listen to the music, hear the words
It says, America you're beautiful
Throughout the USA
America the beautiful,
I love you in every way

Walking Away from the Blues

I made up my mind a long time ago
If you didn't straighten up I'd have to go.

I tried my best to do my part
But you wouldn't do right.
You played with my heart.
You didn't believe what I said.
That my love for you was going dead.

The thrill is gone and you're all alone
Don't cry to me.

Tired of making things go right,
So I finally saw the light
Now that it's over you want to be true.
So long, baby, there is nothing I can do.

You done me wrong,
You're on your own.
There is nothing else I can do.
But walk away from misery.

Walk away from the blues.

Vacation

Vacation is a time to really unwind
So leave the stress and be at rest
Enjoy the summertime.

Each breath of air that you inhale
Relaxes and eases your mind,
With pleasant thoughts of hear and now.

Leave your troubles behind.
This is the time to laugh and play.

A splash in the pool will do.
It's one of the many blessings
That God has afforded to you.

It doesn't always last for long,
So enjoy family and friends
Capture each moment until you meet again.

To Know a Friend

After the moment I met you
Our friendship just grew.
Each day as they passed
I thought of you more often.
Very seldom can you find
A friend so very grand

Who understands your ups and downs
And will lend you a helping hand.

Whenever I need for you to come around
You do not hesitate.

That's part of being a friend
A friend shouldn't have to wait.

To our friendship that we have
May continuously be its growth.
And the love of our friendship flourishes
More and more

Friend, dear friend, how well do you know
The real meaning of our friendship?
As long as life has not to unfold
This is the meaning I'm sending to you.
Since the day our friendship grew.

To Be Black, Courageous, and Beautiful

It's such an awesome thing
Oh look at what joy
Of being that you bring,
To stand up and be able to speak
Intensely to people you meet.

To talk about a plan to solve
The solution of our land
Courage that brings about one's faith
To carry out your dream
And inventions brought to life

Of things you'd never seen.
The day has come, the time is now
With heartfelt tears of joy.
To seek the mind of your soul, to find out
Just how brilliant that you are.

Now that's your stairway to success.
A step you were made to climb
Keep forward, my friend.
And leave your troubles behind.

Just focus on the prize.
Taking one step forward at a time
For to make a difference
In all that's said and done.
Woman, look around.
The battle you have won.

Be Not Dismayed of the Storm

I've sheltered the storm.
I've walked through the falling rain.
But the love I have remains the same.
What good is it to have silver and gold
Without love in your heart,
What good is your soul?

I can feel love in the darkest of the night.
Hold on to another hand and say,
Everything's going to be all right.

I know the darkness of the clouds will roll away.
The sun will shine again and brighten up your way.

Keep looking up and never down
There is a light shinning at the tunnel
When you come through.

No more heartaches. No more tears. No more pain.
There's so much in store, there's so much to gain.

When you believe Jesus will bring you through.
I know. I'm a witness to the whole wide world
Of what my Lord can do.
He will do it again for you too.

Before You Judge Me

Before you judge me
Don't just look at my color
I am human as another.
I have a heartbeat
And a pulse too, you see
I'm just as human as you.
Just because my skin is brown
Don't be so quick to put me down
I'm warm, passionate, loving, and kind.
Someday you might be a friend of mine.
Before you judge me
Remember one thing
All things in life become a change.
I might be one of your kin
I wonder how you will judge me then,
Love has no color, it blends right in.
Judge me not, but let love speak.

When Brown Leaves Fall

When I see fallen leaves
Upon the grass that's green
They don't just lay unnoticed
They create a scene.

The wind sometimes sends a blow
And scatters them around
And even though they are brown
There's beauty to be found.

When the grass is mowed
Some they cultivate and
Those that are turned under
Lie there in wait.

Until the grass grows green again
Then you will never know.
What happens to the fallen leaves
That you had seen before.

The Power of Love

Only love can stop the pain
Of one's such feelings
That heartache can bring.

Only love can be so strong
To give up the right,
When you know that they're wrong.

Only love will see you through
When you know not what else to do.

When you're lonely,
Frustrated, downhearted, and blue
Love is there to see you through.

Love is there beyond the extreme
Always waiting, if you know
What I mean!

Love is always found within,
Through pain and suffering
Love fits right in

Love is there to see you through
And the answer to love lies within you
It's your heart, you see
So be the best that you can be
Love has its way!
Go ahead enjoy your day!

The Mood of Love

Somewhere in the night, I fell in love with you
We danced to the music that said I love you too.
My heart was so excited out on the ballroom floor
The second time around I had to dance once more.

I kept on listening to the words saying, I love you
The twinkle in your eyes led me to the clue.

When the music stopped, the words they still remain.
I said to my heart this is not a game
While still standing there on the dance floor
My heart was pounding fast like never before.

The magic of the night proved my love for you
Once in a lifetime, a love like this comes true
While we were out there, dancing the night away
Love slipped right in and that's right where it stayed.

The Life They Gave

For a life to save to those on land
From the terrorist plan of the Pentagon

They use their cellular phone
To make their final call

To their loved ones and friends
And anyone they knew.

They weren't afraid of the terrorist on flight
They changed their course of plan

Instead of the Pentagon they went down on land

And in their hearts they knew that this day would end

And they would leave behind a loved one or a friend.

And in the twinkle of an eye
Christ would meet them in the sky.

And take them to their home on high, forevermore.

The Courage of the Black Man

Out of the Congo, he has risen to great power
From toiling through slavery of little by the hour

A determination of a change to come
A change in society that will change history

He came out of the foxhole to walk among men,
And to let them know, there is no fear within.

To raise his children and take care of his wife
Is the struggle it's been of a black man's life.

A dream he's hoped for, that the color of his skin
Will not be judgmental of the person within

A change he's prayed for with God's amazing grace
Has brought about a change to the human race

Black man—continue in Grace.

A Highway Called Holiness

In memory of my Mother
Elmira J. Smart

There's a highway we must travel
To enter at the gate.
This road is long and narrow,
And brighter is the day.

This road is not made of fun, or laughter;
Instead it's called Holiness
And the reward is already paid.

On this highway your days
May seem dark as night,
But believe in God Almighty—
He'll lead you in the light.

As we reach out to meet him,
He'll be standing there within to greet you
And never say good-bye.

AMEN

The Path That Leads Me Home

Thinking back on memories,
Today, I walk the trail that I used to go
A path that I once knew
From long, long ago.

The flowers that grew in the field nearby
Brought thoughts to my memory
Those made me stop and cry.

It was the trail that Mama took
To walk me along the way
When my aunt and I visited
And wanted to stay and play.

And when the evening came
And it was time for me to go
I walked the trail that Mama took
And the pathway I would know
That led me home, so long ago.

My Mother's Touch

So very soft and tender
And gentle was the touch
I didn't have to see
I knew it was you, Mother!

So very soft and gentle was the hand that I felt
Touched by you, Mother, as my heart cried and wept.

I knew it was you, when I looked around
No one was in the room,
No one to be found.

Just the gentle touch
Of my mother's hand
An unseen angel.

A Meal to Serve

A meal to serve and a hand to hold
Is such a comfort, I've been told
If I can serve a meal today and
Help someone along the way

If I can pass along a smile
It makes my job worthwhile

If I have done the best I can
Lending others a helping hand

I'm as happy as I can be
Knowing the service came from me

A Christmas Scene

As each house on every street
Glitz with red and green.
What a beauty to behold
The sights of Christmas scenes

Holly berries of Christmas wreath
And lights strung along the way
Soon the hour will come that we
Celebrate our Christmas day!

While little children as they sleep
Throughout the night to dawn
With happy hearts when morning comes
Will know the real true light

Of happy hearts filled with love
And sharing gifts with glow
In every scene Christ is the reason
It's him that we adore!

Keep Christ in your Christmas day
As you go about your way
And have your self a merry, merry
Christmas day

A Many Splendid Dreams

In an unknown land I travel through
A world of many years
Fighting to capture every moment through
Happiness of tears.

I close my eyes and there you are
So close I feel you breathe
I see your face I know your name
Don't ask me how, I can't explain.

Someday I will meet you face to face
I wonder will it be the image in my dream
I saw of you and me.
Traveling many miles away
Throughout unknown lands
Floating softly through the breeze
Holding hand in hand.

How can a fantasy become a dream so very true?
In all my thoughts my wonders are,
Will I love you?

A Moment of the Morning

I awake to the morning
With the question on my mind,
Which way am I headed
And where can I find the answer
To my problems
I face each and every day?

Then I take a moment of silence
And I began to pray.
The changes are amazing
In a twenty-four-hour day
I look to God,
He owns everything,
And to my crowded mind
All the comfort he brings

In a moment of prayer
Oh what peace and joy
Of his love he gives!
Just to look to him
And awake up to live.

A Light at Sea

I took a stroll along the seashore
To watch the ships go by
And drift into the sunset.
How awesome is the air to breathe
As the ships sail slowly by
A thought of remembrance
Brought a teardrop from my eye
I stood there on the shore.
The captain sailed out of sight.
All that was left
Was the lighthouse light.
I know her captain
Devoted to the very end.
Sail on, Your Majesty,
Out there on the blue.
Someday, while I'm strolling along
I'll see you sailing through.

Brighter Day

My days are brighter as I feel laughter
I'm in a world of my very own
I smile within my heart
As I sing this merry song.

It's a new day for me
I'm so happy because I'm free.

Look all around me.
The sun is shining on me.

I'm over the hurt you put me through
I feel so brand-new
All my dreams that you were in
Was an illusion, now that we're through.

A brighter day is here for me.
Because I see myself free from the fantasy of you.

A Wonderful Dream

I saw you in a distance
Of the shadow of my dream
And when I met you face to face
You were the image that I'd seen

Your voice was a whisper
Of what I heard before
The words you spoke so softly
I had heard them long ago!

A New Day!

Today is a new day we've never seen

A blessing in hopes of a challenge and dreams

A place in time that we look to explore
To seek a reason in life once more

To climb a mountain to its peak
And tread in the deepest valley below

It's the strength of Him with the highest power
Who gives the measure of the distance?
We must go each one

All in a New Day

In the very silence of my mind
I pray and am thankful
Of this adventurous day that is now

Caught Up in Your Love

I can see love in your eyes
Feel it in your heartbeat
Can't you see my love?
You were meant for me.

When I'm in your arms
My heart seems to melt.
Caught in all your charm
There love is kept.

I'm feeling really good,
Like never before
Don't leave me now,
Please don't close that door.

Take me to heart, this is all I've got
Captured by your love, we just hit the spot
Boom, Boom, Boom hear my heartbeat knock.

It's funny how real love
Can be the moment I saw you,
I knew you were meant for me.

I'm so excited, give me the love you got
We can sail away and let our love boat rock
Caught up with this heartbeat, me and you.

Columbia—
The Shuttle Tragedy,
Shattered Dreams

Today as we pray and hold each other's hand
Throughout this global land

We feel each other's pain,
For broken hearts and shattered dreams still remain.

So close to home, the courage to go so far away
A mission planned so well,
What could have happened on the trip?
Who could possibly tell
That something would or could go wrong?

On the morning of February one,
Of the entire world has seen,
Another loss has become
Another shadowed dream

Broken heart and shattered dreams
But up above the sky so blue.
There are mansions never seen.
Like stars twinkling in the sky
They're watching you and me.

Life has its journey. Life has its plan.
Life has its beginning. Life has its span.
To enter into another world
They have reached their height
Where life never ends.

A Mind to Use—
A Peace to Find

Beyond earth, pestilence, and war
A mind that seeks beyond the stars
A joy to find Christ in your life so divine

A soul that looks up to the sky
For eternal life by and by

A peace in rest I cannot find
A heavy load I carry.
I have not laid my burden down
I must give up tarrying.

To receive my royal crown
From Christ alone, I'll find.

Crazy for Loving You

Maybe I'm crazy. Maybe I'm weak.
All I can see is you in my sleep.

It's been so long, I'm all alone.
I'm crazy for you.

Day after day, night after night
I sit and cry wondering
Why you said good-bye.

I'm all alone and singing this song.
I'm crazy for you.

You're in my dreams. You're all I see.
We're walking together, just you and me.

I guess I'm crazy or still in love with you.

You made me weak when you said good-bye.
A river of tears flowed from my eyes.
I guess I'm crazy and can't help myself.

It's you I'm loving and no one else.
You're the reason I'm singing this song.
I'm crazy for you.

Echoes in the Night

Echoes in the night I cannot refrain.
I hear a voice keep calling out my name,
And in the restless sleep
I can see the image of your smiling face
Looking at me
Nighttime is not easy
And days seem the same
Echoes in my mind
I hear the calling of your name.
Looking at your picture
Thinking on the past,
How once we laughed and sung together,
Oh what a blast.
Echoes in the night
Will last a lifetime through
'Cause in my restless night all I see is you.

A Night to Remember with You

Where can I go to find peace of mind?
When I'm alone with you?
Somewhere there is a quiet place,
Just between us two.
I just want to hold your hand,
Look into your smiling face.
Gather up all your charm;
Hold you in my loving arms.

One night with you I can fantasize,
Let me live the night.
I get dramatic over you.
Once in a while someone will come along.
The thrill of my heart makes me sing a song.

Just to see you smile.
You don't realize what it meant to me.
I'm happy as I humbly am.

Making honey
So, darling, can't you see,
What this one night is doing to me.
I'm falling in love with you.
And I don't know what I'm going to do
I have just one night with you
And then I'll be alone.

With nowhere to look for someone
As beautiful as you are tonight

A Place in Time

Somewhere in time we've already been
Through the clouds that's dark and gray.
The rainstorm and the wind

We build our faith and hope
On another source above
In Jesus we're sheltered
By His mercy and His love.

When the raindrops stop falling
And wind ceases to blow
We look around ourselves
And the love ones we don't know.

Through our devastation
As lessons we have learned.
To lean on each other
And shelter the storm.

The storm may come again
And the strong winds may blow.
But He who's in control
Knows the way it will go.

Give Him the thanks He's worthy of
All praise lifts Him up and praise Him high.
He'll brighten up your day.

And when the storm returns to you
Be not dismayed.

Things That I Remember

It was a long time ago, but how well do I remember
When my dress was made from a flour sack
And our house was across the track
We raked the yard with a fennel broom,
But the yard was as clean as the living room
Some of the chairs were of an orange crate
But it was a place to sit
We grew up on black-eyed peas,
Corn bread, and collard greens
My father was a fruit picker
My mother was a housewife
For a while, then later worked in the fernery
We all as children worked
To have and learn the value of a penny if any was left
After making provisions for our household
And as family values
Was very proud to be a part of support of each other.
This memory has stayed with me through
All my childhood years
So as of today I can look back on past times
And appreciate my rearing; this has helped
Me to be able to continue
To be devoted and show as well as share love.

Winter Weather!
When It's Cold Outside

The weather is cold outside
And the snow is falling down
But I don't care at all
As long as you're around
Let it snow, let it snow, let it snow

I feel your warmness close to me
And in your eyes I see
The glow of love within you
When you're right here with me
Let it snow, let it snow

I'm wrapped up in your arms
Surrounded by your charm
As long as it's cold outside
Let it snow, let it snow, let it snow

A Silver Lining

Like an eagle that spreads its wings to soar
My spirit tends to rise to grasp the very truth
That appears before my eyes.
I must not doubt my thoughts.
Within I feel the presence is my here and now.
It's where I want to be.
Songs of praise are in my heart
Joy lifts my soul.
Peace, I have as I walk on this rocky road.
My hands are held in faith
I know I will not fall
Because He hears my prayer
And answers to my call

Caught in the Crossfire

These Clouds are dark and dreary
Hanging overhead
The raindrops keep falling
I'm getting soaked and wet
But your voice I keep hearing
Calling out my name
I'm caught up in this crossfire,
Wondering who's to blame

A distance across the miles
Your voice I still hear
I know you're miles away but your
Presence feels so near

I long too see your face and
Feel your warm embrace
But all that's left for me is the
Reflection that I see
Looking back at me from a distance
Caught up in this crossfire
Wondering who's to blame.

A Soldier's Prayer

Lord, on this battlefield I pray
That you will guide me night and day
Be the light to shine for me
So that all the world can see

You're victorious in your plan
All carried, but through the hands of man

To all my loved ones, family, and friends
I'll fight this war to the bitter end

Just like Daniel in the lion's den
He had no fear of them or men

He held on to the faith he knew
And surely, Lord, you brought him through

A Special Sister

Today I'm thinking of you in so many ways.
Of times we spent together,
Throughout our childhood days.

You're the kind of sister
That everyone should know.
And most of all, I want to tell you
How much I love you so.

You're the kind of sister
That I can count on.
And I still do
Even though I'm grown.

A sister like you should know
On this our Mother's Day,
That you're a special sister
And this is a special day.

Happy Mother's Day, Sister!

A Time to Remember

To walk upon the pure white sand
Upon a sunny beach
Such a wonderful delight,
What an awesome treat
To look across the ocean waves
What a sight to see
One of the many blessings
Thou have given me!

How fresh is the air we breathe
As I walk along the way
My inward thoughts, oh how wonderful
You have made mine, this today!

With birds flying in the air
And loved ones all around
It's just a bit of heaven
Here on earth to be found

What great joy is now
And when now has passed its way,
We'll build our hopes and dreams
On what was yesterday.

Enjoy the earth beneath your feet
Reach out and feel the breeze.
Capture the love that surrounded you
Set your heart at ease.

Just imagine Paradise just like this
It's real, this is my say,
Relax in the enchantment of the beach!

A Day at the Beach

Another day of leisure
Out here on the beach
Basking in the sun
Enjoying the summer breeze.

Vacation is for everyone,
Relax,
Take a day, or two
You owe it to yourself
That only you can do!

Joy is everywhere
Hear your heartbeat,
Without the sounds of music,
Or the waves beneath your feet.

Come over and join me
Have a fun-filled day
After you're relaxed,
Go on your merry way.

A Woman among Women

Who's that Lady?

A woman among women is who I am
A woman of color, with long black hair
Eyes that can pierce into the dark of the night
Look into the heart and see into the light.

The IQ I carry may not be much
But I have the intuition to keep in touch
To me the height above me to the level below
And a sense of guidance wherever I go.

Not to be judgmental by the color of my skin,
But to be looked upon, for what comes from within.

To show love and give it
Takes from the strife
This is the joy I get from my life.

Echoes in the Winds

Remain here with me
Flashes of her face
I'll forever see
That's what 9/11 left for me.

I'd give my every tomorrow
To make our dream come true
Now all I ever have
Is your echo saying, I love you.

Echoes in the wind
Thoughts of your touch
We had a love so strong
How could this go wrong?
Echoes in the wind will always be my song.

A Name for Fame

An American Idol born
to be among the many stars.
A Name for Fame.

At last your dream has come along
As you rose to meet your stars
In all the wonders of the world
They know what you are.

An American Idol born to be among the many stars.
You've reached the essence of time and worked real hard to find that
particular place in life to be so proudly crowned.

As the world watches in awesome wonder of the American Idol to be,
I know in my heart you had reached your stars, without the doubt
of a fantasy.

You've searched out your dreams. At last you've really found that
special place that only one could find.
You've soared many heights and now that you know.
You have got what it takes. That's a plus and more.
To dream on the invisible dream takes faith along with courage. You
know exactly what I mean.

To reach the stairway you have climbed was about hard work and a
made up mind, to win your royal crown.
Fame was there waiting with you
With the gift of a voice to bring.

Feelings

Sometimes I feel when I've done my best
I've tried real hard to pass the test.
Toiling to do the best I can
Giving respect to my fellow man
Some folk just don't understand.

Carrying the weight of a heavy load
Trotting down a rocky road.
I must keep going. I cannot quit.
The job half-done will not fit.

With my feeling I will succeed
The goal was hard, but worth the deed.

Now that it's over, I passed the test
I didn't give up, I've done my best.

Find Yourself and Be Known!

Look into the mirror, what do you see?
A reflection of self, ebony
So beautiful in color with the right hairline
Eyes that are bright like a morning star!
Woman of color!
Do you know who you are?
It's never too late to find your place.
We are all part of the human race.
Soul-searching can take a little time,
Once you know you're found
Dreams will flourish one by one
Until your goal is reached and done
Fame and fortune just might be!
With the brilliance and beauty that I see!
When you soar to heights,
To spread your name,
With your silky hair
And smooth brown skin!
From looking good to Hollywood
Your dream will never end.

Another Day in Paradise

With laughter all around me
And the sounds of birds singing in the air
Your body close beside me
Lets me know how much you care
This is just another day in paradise.

To feel the joy of being with you
I'm happy as I can be.
To me this is paradise with you
Right here with me.

Walking with you hand in hand
Know how much I love you
And you're my man.

Oh what pleasure
It is to treasure
Being here with you
To me this is paradise
For the entire world to see.

Good-bye, My Love

If you love me like you say
Keep on loving me in your own way.

For me this is the end
It's all over just call me a friend.
Good-bye, my love
I will get over you one day at a time
It was my dream of making you mine.

You said you loved me, and I tried to believe.
I'm leaving you baby
I'm leaving misery
I'll get over you one day at a time,
I made up my mind.

Baby, I can't take it no more
My heart's been broken too many times,
Go on your way, and I'll go mine
Somewhere in time our aching hearts will mend
Keep in mind love, you can call me friend,
Good-bye, my love.

Hard at Work

I work real hard so I can find,
When I go home a peace at mind.

To enjoy home with the best of things,
Of the money I make and the joy it brings.

It takes long hours and plenty of work,
Just to have an extra buck.

So when I go on a shopping spree,
I can spend my money fancy-free.

A little here and a little there,
Buying pretty things without a care.

And when at night I go to bed,
All these bills won't juggle my head.

In the fashion of my home
I'm content.

Heart and Soul

To release love from the soul
My spirit must be free.
My love I cannot hide
Of it the world must see.
Like twinkling stars in the sky
A million miles away
My love will be shown
In its own separate way.
Soft and gentle
As the breeze of my love
You can feel it coming
From the heart of my soul.

His Light Shined

If you're in the darkness and you cannot see,
Search for a star. There's sure to be one.

With its light so bright, it will lead you.
Which only alone, my God can do.

When you're in doubt and feel in despair.
Be not discouraged. He's always there.

There's nothing alone my God can't do.
What He's done for others that He will do for you.

Cherish His Grace. Believe in His Love.
Trust in his truth. There is life in His Word.
In my Father's house, there are many mansions.

If it were not so, He would not have told you so.

I Never Thought That I Would See the Day

I never thought that I would see the day,
From my love that you would walk away
From me and hurt me this way!
Now that I'm home
I'm all alone without your love.

It's like a ship that takes to the sea
That's how you took your love from me.
Drifting slowly across each wave
Till I no longer see it sail your love
Drifting away from me

These memories keep on haunting me
For your love I miss so much
When I reach out to feel
What was once so real
No longer can I touch.

My heart yearns for your love
That drifted slowly away!
There is so much misery inside of me
I need your love to set me free.
I'm lonely without you, and I will miss you too.

When Shadows Overcome You

When dark clouds overcome you
And the sun doesn't seem to shine
There's a light within you
That's very much divine.

Open the window of your mind
And truly you will see
That the sun is still shining
In spite of what you feel

Enclose your mind with thoughts of Him
He sees you from above
He'll clothe you with warmth
And the tenderness of His love

He feels the loneliness of your heart
And knows your every pain
Lean on Him and know, that in
His heart, you'll always remain.

An Island of My Own

In the middle of the ocean
I can feel the breeze
Captured by the sunset
Set my heart at ease.

I'm going to wipe away my teardrops
Rid my every pain
Caught up on this island
I think I'll remain.

Just to ease my mind,
Relax and unwind
Enjoying the summer breeze
Flowing through the coconut trees.

Every Island has someone
Here is where I'll stay
Until true love comes my way.

Like the raven in the sky
On this island I will die
Never again will I roam
'Cause the Island is my home.

Another Year's End

As 2003 slips away, I'll say a silent prayer.
That God will watch over us
And keep us in His care.

As 2004 is at our door
Another year has gone once more.

Let's keep marching on, for victory
Has its stay when all is said and done.

Broken hearts and shattered dreams
May still yet remain

But in our heart of Him we know
He'll heal our deepest pain.
When the bells ring on New Year's Night

And the stars shine bright, you see
Remember each soul that's gone away
Is watching you and me.

Awakened by Nature

When the storms of life
Approach with an appeal,
It looks like a movie
But you know that it's real.

You know it will come, but which way will you go?
It's a stroke of luck which no one knows.
One day you're here, the next day you're gone
One day you're happy the next day you're alone.

Like the ocean that brings in the tide
Then takes them back to the other side.
Like the clouds that form and bring down the rain
Then the sun shines through and it's dry again.

Sometimes the winds gently blow
Other times they come with a loud roar.
Today is a stage of being within.
Tomorrow you think on where you have been.

A hope for the future of unseen things
While being in the presence you still remain
What joys you partake of the essence of life,
While others follow with heartache and strife.

I Will Not Forget

Never will I forget
The memories of your kiss,
The way you make me feel
I cannot forget
The tenderness of your touch
Because I know it's real
I cannot forget
When I'm a little blue
The little things you do
I cannot forget
The way I hear you say
Sweet little whispers in my ear.
I miss you so much.
To me you are my dear!
All of this I can't forget
Because I love you so
And each day goes by I love you more.
Never will I forget, because I love you.

Moon over the Two of Us

When the moon appears over the ocean
And the reflection of it, there I see.
What else is there to look for, except
The stars above you and me.

So here's to you, my love,
May our dreams forever be true
To every moment that I see your smile,
I'm falling more in love with you.

Enchanting it is just to you and me,
Out here alone on our own
Feeling the breeze from waves as
They pass with a soft lullaby.

When we get married, we'll have a
Celebration down by the ocean,
Just you and me,
There will be a halo around us too,
Just meant for us to be.

Love on the Blind Side

Love on the blind side is when you cannot see
That I am a person and shouldn't be cut down like a tree.

Love on the blind side is looking at one color
When we ought to unite and love one another.

Love on the blind side is when you do not think,
Because you're at the top, but you should never forget
That you could fall within a wink.

Love on the blind side is when you didn't think,
You'd grow old someday, and the least of those you expected
would help you on the way.

Love on the blind side is when you cannot feel
When the heart is true,
And it doesn't matter what color you are.

In the Creation of Color I Find Love

When I look into the black of night
How beautiful is the darkness behind the stars and moon.
Love created it.
By love it was created.

The sun light up the daytime for our need of its light.
Sometimes the clouds are white.
In stormy weather they form gray.

In the rainbow there's pink, yellow, blue, and green.
There's a promise of it.
Do you know what it means?

The sky beyond is very blue
In all the colors presented, which are you?

They are colors of love.
In the pitch of the night of 9/11
All came together and united as one.
Why can't we show love and harmony
Without another tragedy?

We never know just like before when broken hearts
And shadowed dreams,
Will be once more in all the colors I have seen.
Love was embraced on every face.

My Happiness

My heart so true I offered you
A love sincere a love so true

With sunshine mixed with the fallen rain
Through heartache tears, joy, and pain,
With all this love remains.

To prove to you my love was true
My eyes will fill with tears
By the hurt you put me through.

Throughout our golden years
I'll cry no more
My tears are gone
And you're left standing alone,
In a world of dreams
You left to me my happiness.

It's All in America!

Happy faces here and there, sounds of laughter in the air! We are sincere, we do care. It's all found here in America! To walk across ocean waves or walk along the sandy beach, as people pass each other they seem to always greet! How beautiful are the hills and slopes where the grass is green and nature unfolds its wonders of some things we have never seen! America the beautiful, we embrace her with our love! As our flag banner waves in the air beneath blue skies above America, our beautiful colors remain. Never will they be changed from the red, white, and blue! America, America, you're so very grand where we live our dreams throughout our many lands, it's all in America, your dreams to share you can.

Love Will Find Its Way

When the light of love shines on me
And my heart feels the joy
It's like little children running around
Playing with a brand-new toy.

I'm happy all day long
As I hum or sing my song
Because there's nothing to go wrong
When I'm with you.

There is so much love that I feel
And I know that it's real
With you in my life.

When I'm with you
Sun shines at my back door
Teardrops faded away
When I'm with you.

You know that it's true
Never again will I be blue
When you're here with me.

It's You, My Love

When I see your face
I'm caught up in the mood
Turn the lights down real low
Let's get in the groove.

Because it's you I love
What are we waiting for?
This is the moment we both have waited for.
I love you.

Come a little closer I feel your body's heat
Wrap your arms around me set your mind at ease
I love you.

Baby, don't you know what it is to wait
Give me all your love don't think to hesitate

There's no doubt about it, our love is here to stay
If the price of loving you is what I have to pay, I love you!

Lighthouse

Like the lighthouse on the shore,
How bright the light shines.

Little boat sailing,
keep your sail up high,
Rough is the water
as you sail right on by.

I'll keep my eyes open wide
And watch you're every oar,
As you glide right on by.

Bright is the light as you sail right in.
I'm glad to be your neighbor, and
You can call me friend.

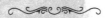

Joy of Life

A little joy a little pleasure
A heart so true in many measures
To seek the gifts of unknown treasures
Is where the true meanings of life are found.

I would not change my colors
For the glitz of the rich
I see before my eyes

A heart as pure as mine,
And a memory to hold
Of the joy a peace I seek to find
In the contentment of my soul

As I gaze at the stars in the heaven
I feel a peace of mind
To know that joy and love
Is the greatest gift of its kind.

My Little World

Small is my world, but big are my dreams
Of things and places I've not seen.
And have opened my eyes to succeed
It's just the beginning of my happiness.
To know who I am and what I can do
Open my cares to new avenues.
You never know your place in this world
When you keep leaping hurdle after hurdle
Success takes over when you're determined
With the people you meet.
Just reading a script from the power of my pen
And the thoughts that flow from my mind within!
Helps others know by knowing my nature.

My Love

My, how my love grows for you
more and more all the little things you do:
so simple, so loving, so unforgettable you.

Deep in my heart there's a yearning
That keeps me longing more of you
Arms that hold me oh so soft
Lips that kiss me tenderly

Oh my love, don't you know.
How you flick my heart.
Stay right here don't go away
because I love you so.

Nighttime seems the perfect time
to hold you in my arms.
Wrap me up in your ever-loving charm.

Together we share a love so true
between you and me,
a love that will last until eternity.

Nothing Remains the Same
A Rainbow in My World

In the stillness of the night
When no one else is around
I lay alone on my pillow
And the tears come streaming down.

The pain I feel inside
It's not for the world to see,
When the morning comes
And the sun peeks through
A new day is coming and the tears I shed
Yesterday faded with the dawn.

When the storm cloud passes over
And the sun begins to shine
The vision of my rainbow
Shows more clearly in my mind.

Look into my world,
I wish that you could see
The colors are so beautiful
Of my rainbow around me.

In a twenty-four-hour day
Nothing remains the same
Every minute of the clock
Brings about a change
In my world with me.

Now That It's Over

It took awhile to believe
How much that I have been deceived?

Now that it's over and the pain is gone.
I know I can make it on my own.

Blue skies and sunshine are what I see.
And I'm as happy now as I can be.

Someday I'll be a real true friend.
That will stand by me until the end.

Your style of life wasn't for me.
So go your way so you can be free,
To do your own will,
Because for me there is no thrill.

Once it's over and said and done.
All of this I'll overcome.
Now that it's over.

Happy New Year

Let It Shine

There is a light that shines on me
For all the world to see
The color of my aura that shines brilliantly
There's happiness on my face and joy in my heart
Patience reproof me to help me do my part
Deep down inside of me Love has a home
Sorrow brings in remorse to let go of my wrong.
Forgiveness is always there to help out charity.
Faith has no doubt of my light for the world to see.
This I pass to you
Take it as a guide; you too will glow,
with this light you cannot hide,
Light of love shine on me!

One Night to Remember

As the darkness appeared
To surround the depth of Night
There appeared the moon
Of a crescent light
The stars were there
In the distance of time
Your eyes were twinkling
As they met with mine.

As we sit and chat
With one another
It was so different from any other
The whispers of your voice so clear
And the feeling of warmth
With you being right near
As your eyes met with mine.

One in a million
Can capture the truth
Of what could be a lifetime,
Of one night to remember with you!

Recognize the Light

As the stars shine around the world
Let us not forget His birth.
Christ our savior, He is the reason
For the celebration of the season.

Gifts of love we share abroad
To let each other know we care. And happy faces all aglow
Show Christ within, wherever we go.

As we string Christmas lights
Along the way
Keep Christ in the reason
We celebrate Christmas Day.

Let Me Be the One

When your day has come to an end
And you're all alone and need a friend
Let me be the one.
With arms wide open waiting on you
Someone you can tell your troubles to.
Let me be the one to whisper sweet things
For you to hear to reassure you that I love you dear
Always with you on my mind
Never being real hard to find
And when the weather is real cold outside
I'll be right there by your side
Let me be the one.
You don't have to worry
Anymore, baby
You can always count on me,
Just let me be the one
To give you tender love and care!

Love! Love! Love!

Love is the need,
Love is the seed,
Love is the flow,
Wherever you go.

Here and now we must share
Show our love tells we care.
Just be kind or give a smile
Soothe an aching heart awhile.

It's not our fault
It's not our cause
But we are now
In it all.

It's just not about me,
It's just not just you,
It's the things of life
That we go through!

The world is full of ups and downs
Sometimes smiles, sometime frowns
Never knowing what a day will bring,
Their sorrow and joy in everything.

Until we reach that other shore
Where the storms of life will be no more
Amazing grace my ear did here
And cause my heart to pound.

Where once I didn't believe
Until I heard the sound!—Katrina.

Old Memories

I have been many places
Through the tracks of my mind
We never thought our love would end
You that I found now.

I am looking back on old memories.
That is what you left
When you took your love from me,
Memories of me smiling at you,
Memories of you smiling at me too
We used to have fun with the best of delight,
But when you left you put out the light.

I'm sitting here with old memories
I think about you, baby, each and every day.
Theses old memories just won't fade away.
It's your memories that I hold on to.
Those memories of me in love with you!

On This Our Wedding Day

What more can I give you
To prove my love is true
What more can I say except
Darling, I love you.

Sweetheart, you're love to me
Is like a rose with the sun
Bursting through the morning dew.

The tenderness of your voice
Thrills me through and through
To you I give this ring,
And all the happiness that it brings
On this our Wedding Day.

I give to you my love
Beyond all prices beyond compare
My vow to you is all my love
Shared on this our Wedding Day.

Silent Mood, Silent Prayer

When loneliness surrounds me
In the still of the night
And I'm heavily burdened
I have silent prayer.

I close my eyes in silence
And pray to the Lord above
In the darkness I can see
The brightness of his light
Of love shinning down on me.

The loneliness I feel
Is no longer here
He fills my heart with joy
And I have no fear.

I close my eyes in silence
And in peace I will sleep
Because he watches over me
And He cares for me.

If I die while I'm asleep
I know my soul to Him He'll keep
Silent mood
Silent prayer.

To the One I Love

To feel the depth of my heart
You must share my love
This is what I offer you
Beneath the stars above

To look into your eyes
And feel the gentleness of your kiss
I'd be in total dilemma
If all of this I'd miss

So here's to you, my darling
On this Valentine's Day
This ring I give to you
For our wedding day
With all my love to you
Happy Valentine's Day, sweetheart!

Happy Valentine's, darling.

Out on the Town

I've been sitting here waiting day after day.
Waiting on happiness to come my way,
But I've decided to go out on the town.
Have a little fun and do some shopping around.

I need a change to forget the past.
The way you're treating me
This love affair won't last.

I need a change to come over me.
And let these down home blues set me free.

I need the sun to shine on me
And the stars to lighten up my night.

The moon bright above me,
And loving arms to hold me tight.

A night on the town just to have some fun
Instead of staying home being the lonely one.
I need a change to come over me.

So I can forget the wrong you've done to me.
Is all I'm looking for tonight.

Pillow Talk Part II

Night after night my pillow is wet
Crying my heart out over you.

The good times we had
When your love was so true
Now you're gone away
And left me so blue.

And I'm still in love with you.

Because my heart won't accept
Baby, you left me for another that's new.

Now can a love affair like this
Continue in my heart to remain?
How come in my sleep at night
I keep calling out your name?

Come on home, baby, and erase this pain.
Don't drive my mind insane.
You know it's me. I know it's you.
Let's stop playing the waiting game.

I'm here at home, so all alone.
Baby, I'm waiting on you.

Return to Me, My Love

Oh my love, I miss you so
My loneliness, you will never know.
So far away from home you've gone now,
I am here so all alone.

As passing days go by
I miss you as I want to cry.
Once I see your smiling face
And in your arm I will embrace.

Until that moment
I'll be missing you
And the love in my heart
Will always be for you
Oh my love, return to me.

Evening shadows fall into
The darkness of the night
Soon another day will be
And you're not home with me.

As passing days go by
I miss you more and more
Oh my love, return to me.
Oh my love, return to me.

Reviewing My Mind

The lesson I have learned
Has really been a cost
My prayer I'm thankful of
Not one soul was hurt or lost.

One drink too many was a plenty
Even though I slept that night
But when the officer stopped me
Alcohol level was still high.

The lesson I have learned
Have been a real high cost
With everything I've gone through
Please don't let this happen to you.

I'm so ashamed of what has been
To me a disgrace,
A scar I put on me for life
That cannot be erased.

To society I offer this
And in my heart it's true.
Don't be a fool and let this happen to you.
Don't drink and drive
Or drive and drink.

It's the simplest thing to do.

Searching out Happiness

When happiness can't be found
Keep smiling and dare not frown
It soon will come
From every smile that you give
Happiness will smile back at you.

And before you know
That you have found
Happiness is there.

Life is not always fair
But one thing is for sure,
And you can count on that
The more love that you give
Will surely multiply
And that's certainly no lie!

Try it for yourself and see if you find
It to be happiness you see,
Because this is the way love is
Bringing happiness to you that will last.

Your heart will sing a song
With a melody that will brighten your day
And happiness will play with your mind
Being mighty kind,
Because of the happiness you have found.

Speaking Words of Wisdom

If you have not wisdom and you have not love
You will never make it to greater heights

For down in the soul it be like a seed
And there it stays till the time of its need.

Love and happiness are all around
Their wisdom you use when you realize they're found.

It's the way to discover the joy within
When you thought you're alone but you have a friend.

It brings the peace you're searching for
Just sum this up and there you are
Words of wisdom are given to you
To help you live a lifetime through.

The Beauty of Them All

The little red bird was a pretty scene
Out there in a field of green
Then he flew from tree to tree
Before he finally recognized me
I admired him as he was there.
He flew away without a care.

I'll look again tomorrow
And maybe I'll see
Him perching on a tree.

Or maybe hopping in the green
This reminded me
Of a Christmas scene.

What a beautiful sight to see
The little red bird, a cardinal

The Blue's Going to Set Me Free

I told you, baby, some time ago
If you don't straighten up
I'm going to let you go.

I tried my best to do my part
But you wouldn't do right
You played with my heart.

You didn't believe what I said
When I told you my love for you was gone
Now you are the one alone
Don't cry to me.

The hope I had for you is gone
I can make it on my own
I told you I loved you from my heart
And thought one time that we would
Never part, you done me wrong and
Now I'm gone, don't cry to me

There's nothing else I can do
But walk away from misery
And let the blues set me free!

I'm setting you free to set me free,
Go on your way forget about me,
You thought I'd be your fool
And never say good-bye,
So long, baby, it's your time to cry
Now that I'm over you
I have a new song,
Good-bye to the blues
I'm free!

The Boundaries of Love

Love has no color. It's a wonderful thing
To the one who captures it.

Oh what love brings
It's a feeling you get when it happens to you
It comes from the heart and you know love is true.

When a man and a woman
Are truly in love
Their eyes twinkle at each other
Like the stars up above

When he gives to her flowers
And the kiss she expects
Love's in the heart
And there it is kept.

So if you're reading these few lines
And I know that Cupid will motivate your mind.

And send its bow straight to you
For this is what being in love will do.

One Is to Love
Two Is to Not Let Go

Many treasures have been found
In many different things
My treasure is found in you, my Love
And all the happiness that you bring.

To you, my Love, who holds the key?
I find in you all the missing links
Of what there is to be.

More than precious gold
Your love for me, all for me
All in one treasure
Deeper than the sea.

Where the Sun Forever Shines

In memory of Millie, my friend

In a land so bright and cheery
Where darkness never comes
No more toiling through this life
When the day is done.

No more pain, no more heartache
No more suffering here for you
Smiles and laughter surround you,
Eternity for you.

Forever joy and happiness
Is surrounded every day
You're toiling is now over
You can run and play.

I'll never forget you
And, too, you're not gone
You just found a place
In a better home.

A friend so grand,
A friend so few
In certainty
Glad I knew you.

Now you're walking the streets of gold
Of the story that's been told.
Where the light and the glory
Of Jesus brightens your way.

What Can I Say?

What can I say to someone out there
Whose heavily burdened and in despair
Someone who's missing
A loved one or friend
By the power of prayer
Your heart will mend.

What can I say when
Your day comes to an end
You'll be sheltered by loved ones
And a host of friends.

What can I say in the
Words that are few
Let the power of prayer
Reach out to you.

What can I say in what has come
Is to have your faith in God's only son
It's the word of God's promise
Keep love in your heart
Trust in his name
He's always the same
And will never change
Jesus Christ the Lord.

This I can say:
Praise his name
Amen.

The Coming of September (9/11)

Through broken hearts and shattered dreams
We hold each other's hand and know
That life has the key to a greater promised land.

Our loved ones who were here before
Have reached the other shore
We too have to understand life's forevermore.

As the tears begin to fall and the hearts faint with pain
The love within our hearts will always forever remain.

September is a month that will always come and go
And as long as the days are numbered the eleventh will be
remembered even more.

So many broken hearts so many shattered dreams,
So much to be thankful for that we still have not seen.

Lord, I thank you now for the days that have come
And gone in truly blessings for me and family on that
September morn.

Praise God.
Good morning, America

A Moment of the Morning

I awake to the morning with a
Question on my mind
Which way am I headed,
And where can I find
The answer to my problems
I face each and every day?
Then I take a moment of silence
And I begin to pray
The changes are amazing
In a twenty-four-hour day.
I look to my God,
He owns everything,
And to my crowded mind
All the comfort he brings
In a moment of prayer
Oh, what peace and joy
Of his love He doth give.
Just to look to him
And awake up to live.

After the Storm

In a world of uncertainty,
We live in hope that our dreams are fulfilled,
Which are sometimes at different times of our lives.
Sometimes the tides of our lives are overwhelming,
To the waves of our mind's eye
We must keep our faith the centerfold of our lives,
And to know that we have an all-seeing God,
Who knows that although the sparrow has no home
He shelters it through life.
How great and mighty is our God,
That knows each of us one by one.
I'm in great hopes that we take a different look on life
And be exceedingly thankful and love our neighbors
As ourselves, to live in harmony of the joy of one another,
That it be pleasing in his sight.
As we look up toward the heaven
We can still see the sight of the rainbow in the sky
And with loving arms we reach out to comfort
Each other through this act of nurture
Can help us as we take hold and grow closer
in the unity of love that we sometimes fall short of
Look back from one to another through devastation
To a flowing stream of love
That awaits us one to another
To be strengthened by God's almighty blessings
After the storm

Sharing the Gift

If I could share a million gifts
The first one would be
The love that surrounds me
Without a Christmas tree!

A twinkle of one child's eye
And the glow upon his face
Sparkles the love within my heart
That a Christmas tree can't replace

My heart goes beyond these measures
Of my Christmas tree of treasures
Our soldiers are not forgotten
However faraway
For our sick and elderly, you too
Are kept in mind with prayer

Picture your tree with gifts
Of this kind of love
With the most precious gift of all
Our Savior Jesus Christ, from him all gifts come.

Sounds of the Children

As the children throughout the world
Gather here and there
To sing the Yuletide songs
Of offerings and of prayer

May their joy be remembered
As each passing day goes by
As their glorious sounds of praise
Sends echoes in the heavens

May peace on earth
Abide with us
As we celebrate the day
Of Jesus Christ, our Lord
To whom we kneel down to pray

Teach the children
Of his love
And his holy name
And in their heart and mind
He will always remain

As the season ends
And a new year begins
Let everlasting love abide
Because love has no end

Viewed by the Judge

A woman appearing before the judge

To my surprise as the verdict was read
The judge looked on
Not a word was said
Then he replied,
What is your plea?

My lips are sealed

For now your charges have been dropped
See you on judgment day,
Said the judge

Breathe

It takes happiness to bring
A smile that's real
Then joy and laughter you will feel

You must forget the hurt that
You felt yesterday of the
Heartache and pain

Let your tears fall like the rain
And wash your hurt away

Your strength will come when
You can see how deep the
Valley is below that you grasp
To reach the mountaintop
From what you've seen below

When you hold on to love, your
Mountain will become a wayside

That flourishes green grass and a
Still stream of water flows
And you can relax
By the trickling sounds
Of its waters in the coolness of the day
And your heart can feel the joy of
Contentment
Of your mind at peace

To a Wonderful Mother

I am glad that you are my mother
Because you're one of a special kind,
A jewel so rare and charming,
And very hard to find.

A mother is someone that you can count on,
A friend who won't let you down,
When no one else is around.

When you send her flowers
She will cherish them and know
That the beauty they behold
Is that you love her so!

Mother, I'm sending flowers to you
For your special day
And you're loved by me
in a special way.

You Were Always There

You were always there when the chips were down
You were always there too soothe my frown
You were always there when I couldn't believe,
And you brought out the very best in me,
You were always there

On you my happiness depends
You were right
There when I needed a friend
When distance came it didn't matter
How long the road to travel,
You were always there
I knew I could depend on you

Your smile I'll forever see,
To hold on to each memory
Remembering of you only the best,
You were always there,
You were always there.

Beauty in the Tree

As the peacock perched on the branch
Looking down below

What admiration of his feathers did flow?

A picture to see how awesome how grand
When he shows the world the color of his fan

Only in the beauty of nature can you find
The sight of this creature to keep in mind

Whether he perches or struts as he's on the go
The proudness in him and that
You will know of a peacock

Secrets of the Waters

Still waters, when you run deep
What are your secrets that you keep?

When you take them down below
Will to the bottom they will go?

Or will they rise when the morning comes
Or will they lie till the day is done?

While ducks float like lily pads
And nature scenes of the wet grass

Still water will you keep
All your secrets in the deep

Feeling Cut Low

Today I'm like a flower
When pruned and lowly cut
But from the strength it gives to me
I know I've got my guts.

Slowly I will grow and every stalk
I'll get so now I must not worry
My blooms will come late
And once again my color will show
In every way.

I slowly gain my strength to have
The height I need in every limb.
My length has grown tall
From whence I was once pruned,
But I've gained my strength to keep living.

True Confession

Sweetheart, once again I must
Confess my love of you.

Here in my heart there will always be you
Through tears and joy
Laughter and pain
A place in my heart you will remain.

But here's to a special day
I want you to know, so I must say
How much I love you,
And you'll always be mine.

Here's too you, darling,
You're my valentine
Today, I give my love
To you always!

My Favorite Spot

Reclining in my chair looking at the ocean
Of the changes come and go with the
Waves that still my emotions

The glisten of its water with the sun beaming down
Oh what a peaceful sight too look upon and find

People walking along the beach
Some bathing in the sun
Little children playing,
A place for everyone

What a perfect place to be,
Just to have some fun
Longboat Key beach a beautiful
Place to be in Florida

Showing My Love

A smile that gives a warm welcome
Shows my love

Hello, how are you today?
Shows my love

What can I do for you?
Shows my love

Here is a drink of water to quench your thirst.
Shows my love

Are you hungry, I'll feed you?
Shows my love

Do you need a helping hand?
Shows my love

Take my hand and lean on me.
Shows my love

These are a few signs of my love
There are so many more.
Can you, or will you, show me
Some of your love signs
To make a more beautiful world
In which we live?

It's the one thing we can share
Freely and let love grow as we notice
The flowers in bloom
What joy love unfolds.

Never in My dreams

I have many dreams and
Some do come true
But never in my dreams
Was me loving you.

Now that I've met you
My dreams no longer come
I guess it took your magic touch,
Because you're the only one.

Every now and then
True love will come along and
Bring the music to my ear
Of real love song.

I'm so excited about how you come about,
And brought a rainbow in my world
When the storm clouds roll away.

Many dreams I had,
And many dreams came true
Never in a dream had I of me loving you.
I'm glad you're here and the dreams no longer come,
I'm so in love with you and you're the only one.

Another Chance on Love

Baby, give us one more chance on our love
We both know our circumstance
Baby, before you close the door
I don't want to see you go
I need to really know,
That you're still in love with me.

Show me tell me, baby, can't you see
I've just got to feel your touch
Because it's you that I love so much
Just give us one more chance on love.

We just need to try again;
I know that we truly can.
Before we take this separation
Out of love and desperation,
We can work it out, before you take off your ring,
We both feel each other's pain
Darling, give our love another chance we can renew
Our romance, with one more chance on our love.

Mother Dear

The most precious jewel
In all the world
That has been given to you
A name so sweet to hear
As my mother dear.

If you have a mother,
Count your many blessings
And those who do not
I'm sure you've learned a lesson.

Talk to her and love her
Keep her in your care
When things come between you
Take it to the Lord in prayer.

In all your endeavors
Love your mother.

Happy Mother's Day.

Enjoy the Moment

Enjoy the moment, take a look around
Skies are blue the clouds move across
Drifting slowly as they go
The breeze blows briskly as it flows

Sunshine peeks through every now and then
But yet there is so much more
That will come when you least expect
That it's all over, you ain't seen nothing yet
There's more, and more, and more

The Run of the River

As water flows down the river stream
A reflection of the sun that shines
Gives to the river waters a soft warm glow
As to mirror the tint of a rainbow
While wildflowers bloom along its riverbank
Unfold scenes of beauty the mind would never think
Gathering pictures of such delight
Now soothing to the mind and soul
Breathing in each breath of air
As the wind blows gently through the trees
I find my mind at ease of such peace
In quietness of nature's wonders
As the river flows endlessly

Mending the Pain

The pain no longer hurts
And tears no longer fall
'Cause I've gotten over you
And that's what I recall.
The sun is shining down upon me
And misery has lost its hold
Now I'm free.

Free to live and love
Singing in the rain
Oh how happiness within me remains
Caught up in a world of my own
Faraway from all the misery and harm.

I'll wipe my eyes of tears that I've shed for you
And gather up some joy to share
Of a life that once was blue.

American Woman, I Love You!

You know I miss you very much
I miss you every day
In the silence to the Lord I pray
Take care of the children and her too
Bless the day this war is through
American woman, I love you!

I'll fight this war 'til the bitter end
Upon me you can depend
The love I have and the love I give
Is all about you
And in the land we live!

Here in America,
Our dreams can come true
American Woman, I love you!
A land of sunshine and skies so blue.

Celebrate the Day

A day for two
Just me and you
Sharing the love that's embedded inside
With each beat of our hearts
It can't be denied

So here's to you, darling, as
We celebrate this day
May our love continue to grow
In its own special way.

For you there's so much love
I want you to know
Seven days a week
My heart to you I show
Forever my love.

May our love life remain
Sharing whatever comes
The heartache or pain
Take time out and celebrate today
With all my love to you.

Time Changes Things

I love you even though I know
How you feel about me
That's what hurt me so,
But I will keep on loving you
No matter what you put me through,
Because time changes things.

I've seen the raindrops fall
And felt the breeze blow through the trees
I've seen the sunshine through
And still my world seems misty blue.

But that's all right with me;
I'll just wait and see,
What the end will be
I know time changes things.

Soon the hurt will fade away
Because my love is here to stay,
I know it'll be a brighter day for you and me
Just you wait and see.

Time changes things
If you believe in prayer
And you truly care for me
Changes in time will come.

If You Only Knew

If you only knew the tears I've shed for you
The times I wish for you and your
Happiness too
If you only knew what you put me through
What would it matter
If you only knew.

If you only knew deep within my heart
I know the answer
To your aching heart,
If you only knew my prayers I have for you;
That Christ will feel your pain
And take care of you,
This is my prayer
That I want you to know
I will always love you and that's for sure
Even through a broken heart
If you only knew
How much I love you.

Someone to Love Me

I need someone who really cares
Someone I know that will always be there

I need a hand to have and to hold
Someone who understands in days of old

Someone I can call in the middle of the night
And need not to wait on the dawn's early light

Someone who loves me and is very kind
Someone who understands my mind

Someone who will always be true
Someone I need, my love is you.

Jesus Is My Light

Jesus is my light,
For the world to see
When I am in trouble,
He will set me free.

Jesus is my light,
Can't you look and see
All the joys that I posses
He has given me.

Hold His hand and don't let go
Let Him be your guide
You'll find shelter from the storm
In Him you can abide
Quiet is the storm with peace.

To Find Joy Within

To find a place to be alone
It doesn't matter where
Just to find peace of mind
And know He hears your prayer.

Tell Him all your troubles
On them He will attend
And move your mountains one by one
He has the strength to open doors
When darkness covers you
Keep your faith in Him alone
He will see you through.

Search not for tomorrow, for
When the day is done
All your hopes and fears
Of your battles are already won.

Lean on Jesus and never doubt
Because He cares for you
He will bring you out
Be at peace, my friend
Wait on the Lord.

Just to Know

When you look up and see the sky,
All is well.
When the tears shed from when you've cried,
All is well.
Love covers a multitude of things,
That makes every thing good
And hurt vanishes like the sun
That burst through the rain clouds,
All is still well.

For little that He knows,
All has been well all the time
We must search our soul and live
Our dreams to be real
And again we will know how
Well all is.

In the midst of a gloomy day,
All can be as well.
As the mist disappearing over the ocean,
Our lives still remain well
With each thought that is given.

A Mother, A Daughter

A mother's love given at birth
A daughter to hold close at heart
A relation to grow, as you take your first step
All coming from your mother's help
Hugs and kisses
Someone who is not a plastic toy
But to feel, hug, and bring plenty of joy.

A daughter, what kind will she be
Will she show love and be kind to me?
Or will she forget in my golden years
The joy of what we shared
Through laughter and tears?

Or will she remember on her birthday
Those precious gifts that came her way?

To show the meaning of a mother's love
A special gift from God above
Always remember your mother.

A Happy Day

As the sun shines so brightly
And birds begin to chirp
As they fly back and forth
Among the trees, how pleasant
Is the breeze you send
As I take in each breath of the freshness
Of your air I'm truly blessed of this day.

And when your clouds bring forth the raindrops,
How clean is the feel of the air?
Given by nature's breath of freshness
Make it to a happy day

As evening begins to fade
Into a sunset so beautiful
It makes the day more enchanting
As I look at all the many wonders
Of what happiness can be all in
One day makes it worthwhile
Being happy and having a happy day.

Captured by the Beauty

When flowers grow by the wayside
And bring forth blooms in the spring
And you hear the chirp of the birds as they begin to sing
The trees tend to bow and the breeze softly blows
As nature takes its place we watch the green grass grow
What beauty there is for the eye to see.

There is so much more to be seen if you'd just let it be
The bees they know each flower
And the pollen that it gives
How precious do they find what help for them to live
Treasure the sight of each one that you see
For this is part of love,
That thou have given unto thee the beauty they behold
Flower in a field or by the wayside as they grow.

America the Beautiful—My Song

All through the street
You can hear the music play
It's my song they're playing
Of the USA.

America, you're great
America, you're loved
It's my song they are singing
All over this world.

Happy, happy people up and down the street
Waving to the USA of every one they meet
All over this world you can hear
The music play.

Listen to the words, hear what they say,
America, you're beautiful,
America, you're grand
It's my song they're singing all over this land.
"America, the Beautiful" is my song.

Be Thankful

To awake and look through
A hole at the sky
Be thankful, for some
Know not when they cry.

Be thankful, for the day that ends
Turn your tiredness into fun
Laughing with family and friends
And all the others that fit right in.

After all it's the joy it brings
Being thankful for the little things
Showing love that we care.

And when we sit down to feast
Don't forget to release,
The thankfulness that we have
Before we begin to grab
For the turkey and the dressing.

Let's thank God for our blessings
On this Thanksgiving Day!

My Sister

Today, I'm thinking of you in a special way

And want to show my love for you
And celebrate your day.

So often we get busy and don't keep in touch
But I want you to know, I love you very much.

I thought to send you flowers
But your garden I help you grow
When you look at them
I know that you know.

And then I thought a card
I'd buy to send for your day
But instead, I thought I'd write these words
It would not say.

You're such a special sister, one of very few
Who demonstrates a sister's love especially like you.

So here's to you on your day
Just have fun, go out, and play
No doing laundry, cooking, or cleaning
Just have fun, eating, shopping, and laughing
And bathe in the excitement of relaxation.

The Proudness of a Peacock The Echoes of the Mockingbird Sound

As the peacock looks back at
Its tail of feathers so proudly colorful
What beauty shows of it
Clothing to be carried, unfolding a showcase.

Sometimes it displays a beautiful fan
Of radiant colors given by nature to this proud creature
As it proudly struts to show
Such glamour to the surrounding of beings
Unchangeable to its stage
As with the sound of the Mockingbird
With the splendor of its echoes
Brought in to nature boundaries
To be seen and heard by the human eye and ear
How great the admirations
That goes far beyond one's imagination
Of beautification through the windows of nature

It's Worth the Battle

Deep in my soul there is warmth
That melts my heart from pain.
Joy, Peace, Love, and Happiness,
Come from calling on His Holy Name.

Prayer does give us strength
To do our golden deed
Keep marching on my friend
Someday you will see.

A smile upon his face
A handshake he will give
A long white robe to wear
A lifetime of eternity to live

It's all worth the battle
That you have gone through
It can't be sold or bought
Nor taken away from you
He has paid the price
His promise he holds true
A life to live forevermore
Which only He can do

Don't Batter My Love

Don't batter my love, just let it be
Don't try to coat or season me.
I'm so delicious you will find
A rare taste that's sweet and kind

There's more to me you won't regret
That you have not even seen yet
To hunger for this love of mine
Is a true confession you will find

Like a pina colada on a fun-filled day
The taste so scrumptious
You'll want to stay
Sweeter than the grapes from the
Napa Valley vine

Your love could be a taste of mine
Aged to perfection waiting on you
From the first taste
Of the best of the brew
Sealed and stocked for the best of all
Labored and waiting until you call.

A Dream to Remember

An imaginary thought of
Someone like you
Can be so real
And not be true
I'd seen that smile
Upon your face
My heart knew
Who you were
When you appeared like in
My dream
You came like a song
That echoed sweet sounds
That could be heard all around
A touch as gentle as the
Morning breeze
I will never forget.
Then you vanished like a shadow
Just as you came, you went
Only to be captured by a
Beautiful dream

You Rocked My World

Baby, it's not easy getting over you,
Because you changed my world
From misty to blue

You brought sunshine into my life again,
Eased my troubled mind and moved the pain,
Baby, I never thought we would part.
Now it's you that's got a pain in my heart,
Because you rocked my world the first day we met,
It's all about you that I'll never forget.

Baby, we had a love so strong,
What caused it to all go wrong?
It's all about you, baby.
I'll keep all these memories of you and me,
'Cause, baby, it was your sweet loving
That had a hold on me.

You rocked my world.

You Changed My Life

You changed my life that I live in
And on your love I did depend
You were there for me to call
I wasn't afraid of the darkness at all.

Somehow, my love, I must go on
And in my many dreams
You're always drifting through

Sometimes I sense to hear your voice
And the echoes of its sound
Lasting hours and hours even though
You can't be found

In the changing of my world
You entered in.

My Friends

My friends think I'm a nut
And maybe it's true
But a nut is extraordinary
And very, very few

My friends think I'm good, good
And maybe that's true
But being a friend is
What a friend will do

I'm filled with fun
And I get upset sometimes
But one thing for sure
You can keep in mind
In me you will always find
A friend, my friend
You'll never forget

The Beauty of a Rose

When you see a rose
In case you didn't know
The deepest of its petals
Show you love the most

Because until it unfolds
You have only seen its bud
So when you receive a rose
The expression it portrays
Is that I love you
In a special way

Take the occasion
Graciously
Enjoy your very day
Because of this rose
To you
My love it does portray.

If My Pillow Could Talk

If my pillow could talk it would tell of my tears
I've cried over losing you, and you would know
In your heart that my love is real and the pain
That you put me through.

If my heart was a mirror that you could look into,
You could see how you shattered my dreams

And on my pillow with all my love there
Your name would be found
This is the way I feel in my heart,
I can't get you off my mind.

What's your plan, baby? Don't say it's maybe
We can straighten this love affair out
And on my pillow these words you will hear
Saying softly without a doubt
My Love for you is so true!

Greetings of the Season

As the sounds ring out of Christmas bells
And lights of color begin to glow
'Tis the reason of the season that
We celebrate to show.

This Glorious Christmas day
To Christ our savior, Jesus
Of Him we kneel and pray.

May peace on Earth be to all
Mankind remain among us all
For one by one He knows our name
He's Jesus Christ Our Lord.

As smiling faces glow,
Let His love abide
And to the world we show love
We cannot hide.

As your holiday is filled with cheer
May your Christmas be bright and
The love of Christ be within our hearts.

Too Hot, Baby

You got that kind of love
That sets my soul on fire.

You're too hot, baby
I want to take off all my clothes
You're so hot, baby,
I'm hot down to my toes.

Baby, you drive me insane
You got me talking to myself
Calling out your name.

You're just too hot for me
I've got to get away
Find myself a nudist beach
And stay there all day.

I need the ocean
And I need the ocean breeze
To take a dive into it
And set my mind at ease.

A Little about Love

Love travels without a bag
Love comes without a tag
Love expresses its meaning
It doesn't have to brag

You can't change love for money
The price you can't compare
Money can only buy you things
Love expresses your cares

If money was the only thing
In this world you could find
Would there be a need
For love one of a kind

Money helps in situations
Love has no limitations
Love will always remain the same

Love does not differ in thought
Instead it seeks to find life
Solutions with meanings

I love you, because money is not
The only reason that I'm here

Company of Three

Company of three was one too many
So one left, two as plenty
One of the two was unhappy
So one left one and went on its way
For one to find a better day

Along the road one went alone
Heavenly burden singing a song
One day you will miss me
Just wait and see
And then you will wish
It was you and me

But I'll be happy
Just being alone
One doesn't fight by himself
It takes two

Windswept

She had the beauty of a
Caribbean Queen
Her eyes dazzle like the sunbeam
Her hair was waving in the wind
The way she looked you could
Call her sin.

She was too beautiful to be true
Her eyes' fashion was of hue
To look at her took a breath of air
She had a walk like she didn't care.

Stacked like a brick, what a chick
If she had to go to jail
I think the judge would drop her bail,
Windswept will come again
I know your name, but I call you sin.

Goldsmith and His Truck!

I'm a trucker, baby, from my heart
You knew this before we started
I love my truck and I love you too!

While climbing mountains
And hills so green
Looking at those pretty scenes
With one thing on my mind
It is getting back to you on time.

Five days on the road, with two in town
Close to my truck is where
You will find me sleeping in my bed
With visions of you running through my head.

When Monday rolls around,
My truck and I are highway bound
With you in my heart, and my gear in my hand
Making this run as hard as I can.

With flashes of you I can't erase
Me and my truck we got a race
I'm coming home to you, baby
Once again, me and my rig.

Welcome

In the midst of the storm
When your troubles seem more
Than you can bear,
Take them to the Lord in prayer.

He knows your heart and in Him only,
Can you find the peace
To erase your troubled mind
Whom only He can see you through,
It doesn't matter of the time.

He knows your thoughts,
He knows your mind.
Life may not at all seem fair,
But trust in Him because He cares.

No matter how the storm might roar,
He stands their at an open door,
Waiting on you to invite Him in
In Him you'll find a mighty friend

He'll heal your broken heart,
And mend your shattered dreams,
That might have been.

There's no mountain peak too high,
No place on earth too low,
No river too long or ocean too wide,
For Him to listen to your call

No night too dark for His light to shine,
A constant friend He is, reach out and touch,
Feel His spirit rise.

The brightness you will see,
A love that cares, a love to share,
For the whole wide world to see,
No matter how bad the storm might be.

Always Thinking of You!

I'm always thinking of you
Of the little things you used to do
It all seems to flash back again
Your smile I see of you and me
Looking back on memories
When you brought sunshine
Into my life
And a smile upon my face
Oh how happy were the days
Thinking of you

Nighttime

To be clothed in the beauty of darkness
Covered by the night
Only to find the two of us
Holding each other tight.

You were meant for me
I was there to be
There in your loving arms
As the dawn's early light
Unfolds her blanket of the night
While being in its cover.

Our heart remains as one love.
As morning radiates the sunshine
And puts gladness into another day
As we embrace the light of Love.

Beautiful Place

Florida—a beautiful place to be
A day sunny with sky so blue
With pillars of clouds drifting
Here and there
The wind it sends a gentle breeze
As it shifts through the trees
What a joyous day to be
Full of fun and fancy-free.

Basking in the evening sun
What a joy, oh what fun
A walk along
The sunny beach
Greeting people as we meet
With birds flying in the air
They don't seem
To have a care.
As we go about our way
We look back on yesterday
We've weathered
The storms and the rain
And picking up the pieces that remain
After all the storms have gone
Florida is still a place of fun
Founded here called paradise.

In All Things, Give Thanks

In all things, give thanks
Who knows what change will bring.
In things, give thanks
Who knows what a day will bring.
In all things, give thanks
Be not selfish within,
Frown not give a smile
You just might find a friend
In all things be thankful
It's better to give than to receive.

What Happened?

Once, we were best of friends.
What happened to us?
Did we lose our friendship because of a fuss?

Once, we were neighbors
But then you moved away
Where are you now?
Where do you stay?

Once, we could talk about anything
Through tears or laughter or pain
Whatever the change
Does any of this remain?
What happened?

To Be Content

Oh my restless soul must find
Peace somewhere within
Will comfort ever come?
From whence it once has been

I need a rest within my mind
Where stillness can be found
Oh if only could I be
Somewhat like a lily
Upon the pad that floats
And lie there upon the deep
With pleasant memoirs to keep
Until the morning comes.

Take Care

Take care of your elderly, treat them with care.
Everybody in this world will need someone somewhere.
Be kind to your parents
Love them with all your heart.
It's God's gift to you until they depart.
He'll gather them up around his throne.
No heartache and suffering,
No living home alone.
Call them in the morning,
Call them at night.
The least you can do is make sure they're all right.
You don't miss your water until your well runs dry.
And they're somewhere beyond God's heavenly sky.

In Search

I took a scroll along the seashore
To watch the ships go by
And drift beyond the sunset of the sky
How awesome it is to watch the
Ships go sail
But sad to know your captain has
Slowly drifted away.

So far across the sea
Into the deep of blue
I wonder if its sail will return
To you

True is her captain devoted to the end
Sail on, Your Majesty,
Out there on the blue
Someday while I'm strolling,
I'll see you sailing through

Talking to the Master!

When the world around you seems upside-down
And the help you need you cannot find

Look to the hills where the sky is blue
He's right near to bring you through.

He will heal your broken heart as well
And on the mountaintop you can go and tell.

He has the key to the bank
Just give Him praise and give Him thanks!
All this He'll do for you,
Just lean on Him He'll see you through.

When your world seems upside-down
Look to Jesus and you will find
A silent listener He's always their
When you seek him in prayer.

From the Author

Words of Inspiration from the Power of My Pen is a collection of poetry written by Earnestine Smart. The poems are about nature, love, family, and current events, as well as the pain and sorrow found in our daily lives. These words are meant to inspire understanding and forgiveness then penetrate the heart with happiness. This collection of poetry was written over many years.

I developed a love of writing poems as a young girl. It is a gift that comes and goes. I take no credit for the words. They are not from me, but just an expression of feelings that flow through me from the Lord.

As I explore how wonderful this gift of poetry is, it stirs my emotions. I am able to forgive and accept vitalizing strength. I go on writing and recapture the beauty it beholds. Then it is released in its many different ways, the words support, prick, sing, and smile as it recreates many thoughts of now, as well as past times. Forming pictures that rise and fantasize as one looks back.

I hope that every reader will find something to soothe the mind and release feelings from the heart. As you recapture inner feelings, this poetry will find a way to be free and live among us. Relax to its entertainment, as its invasion is so graciously accepted. I thank each of you!

Dear Reader
  Thank you for choosing
Words of Inspiration from
The Power of my Pen
  I hope you find joy
in my Poetry

            Love,
            Ernestine Smart